D1006731

SAM'S WORLD

SAM'S WORLD

Poems by Sam Cornish

DHP

Decatur House Press
Washington, D. C.

FIRST EDITION

Grateful acknowledgment is made to the following publications in which some of these poems have appeared: *Berkshire Anthology, Blacksmith Anthology, Cardinal Review, Far Exit, Hanging Loose, Liberator, Natural Process Anthology, Poetry Review, Red Pencil.*

"Women Walk Because," "Fannie Lou Hamer," and "Harriet Tubman's Song" were published as broadsides by the Follow Through Project of the Education Development Center, Newton, Massachusetts.

"Working Until You Are Middle Age" and "I Give What There Is to Give" appeared in a chapbook, *Sometimes,* published by the Pym-Randall Press.

The author expresses his special thanks to Louisa Solano of the Grolier Book Shop for her interest in this collection.

LIBRARY OF CONGRESS CATALOGING
IN PUBLICATION DATA

Cornish, Sam.
    Sam's world.

    SUMMARY: A collection of poems by a contemporary writer.
    [1. American poetry]   I. Title.
PS3553.068S2   811'.5'4 77-3868
ISBN 0-916276-03-1

Decatur House Press, Ltd.
2122 Decatur Place, NW
Washington, D.C. 20008

CONTENTS

To my wife, Florella

and to the Tervalons
for being a family in the sixties

SAM'S WORLD

THE PICTURES OF MY MOTHER

the pictures of my mother
never look like me
they are my ancestors with
an apron full of
beans a mouth ready to sing

i am still trying to hear those voices

I KNEW A MAN

i knew a man
who never read a book
never read a word
but he could sing
he could pick up a guitar
and sing
and he never read a book

he sang of the
south
of leaving home
never having
a home
of women
he never kept
of women he loved

everybody said
everybody
said he knew a lot
and he never read a book

one day he heard a song
he knew
he heard a song
he knew
and knew someone
had heard him sing
had heard him sing

and sang his words
and sang his words

SWEET PEA

some people can see a book
about children praying in the rural south
who cannot buy milk
some people can see sweet pea thank
god for food
her own food worked from the ground
the same food they had the day before
endless taste offering itself
to the body

some children are books because they are
black
and sit on grandfather's lap

grandfather with his coveralls up to his neck
living alone on his farm
talking about church
white men he knew as a boy
the swimming places he will never see again
his daughter washing her children in hot water
heated on a wood stove

his grandchild sits under a tree
wanting to go to the sixth grade
a dry body in her mother's house dress

Sweet Pea is a book of photographs and text for black
children. The poem is a reaction to the pictures and what
the text fails to say.

MY FATHER

my father
brings
me gifts
of melon
nuts
apples
parched
corn
tasted
better in the cabin
my father
stole away
stole away
north

my grandfather
gave his son
a bag
of parched corn
told
him to steal
away
prayed
to god
or gods who
lived
in africa
to
let my father
steal
steal away

my father
sang
the songs
of slaves
of friends
of families
my father
sings
no more
my father
stole
away

GRANDMOTHER'S TABLE

grandmother's table does not welcome
me   she serves tea to sidney poitier
in her house i am not family or in law

in her house her husband's guns
stand by the door seasons into
years locked and put away

her father's slaves your grandmother's
live in maid shadows between us   near
his guns   breaking bread   cookies to please
a woman ninety one   i end her holiday

with a lie a truce and silence

locked guns and cookie molds
books a colored live in maid
the things of an old woman's house

the damp of three bathrooms
the open walls of a long house
nightgowns made for the wind
to creep under and around the body

when i am here once a year
she looks the same
the house the furniture the half
glass of beer

the things of the house
the years of her life

HER FACE IN THE STREET

her face in the street
she looks like the woman downstairs

the shoes belong to someone else
are scattered in the grass
lost in the park

her feet watch me from the holes
in stockings
from the cold lie still

perhaps she fell with a bottle
in her pocket
maybe
the body is dead
is poor

she looks like a woman i have always known

there is a policeman in the street
trying to look like a man

afraid of his car

MOTHER IN LAW

i told you
she would be at the cabin window
beginning to read

hair a threaded gray
spread thin by comb
saying
       good morning

playing with
the cat
& not a word misplaced
in her mouth

you must look at her
hands before you know her
keep the words until

you know
what the lines & flesh
mean and say

to you

THE BLUES

"when she cries inside her body she sings"

she sings
a woman in the streets
the last cigarette
or the night goes on
or the train is coming back
or the train is coming back
and my baby
i have dreamed of
in many places
is coming back

whatever she sings
words are like bread in her mouth

BEFORE I CAN SLEEP AGAIN

before i can sleep again
before i can say i love you

subways will be filled with gas
children hidden in bags of flour

before i can go home
the george washington bridge will rust

the holland tunnel will seal off new york

before you sleep
trains will leap rails plowing farmlands

telephones will keep families
warm through winters

WORKING UNTIL YOU ARE MIDDLE AGE

doing what you dislike
every day wondering about your work
perhaps able to do what you think you want

at my typewriter i think of you
writing i touch you   the days never come
when we understand each other
meeting only to be content
we avoid other problems

you talk of cuba and women's rights
i complain of traveling in america
of the coffee and pistol on the back seat
of the car   listening with your back

we question what is between us
literature that hides my walls behind books
and prints
the talking of people with different values

the country where you live is brown and bare
quiet enough for you to live
but the family you care about you think i will
question and dislike

your parents will enter another life
i ask you to rise out of yours
as i have left mine somewhere
in cambridge thinking of you

PHYLLIS AND ZERALDA

we touch death
in different places

the dead wear heavy
army overcoats

your dog has
long hair &
so have
you

my children
like to eat
dry green
paint on window
sills

a hunter
is a white man
with a red
hat
who kills
hair
dogs and deer

SLAVE SHIP

wrist & ankle
chained
kept
old & still
in the hold
six hundred
standing
between decks
in irons
the dead
and the living
into two
rows
horse beans
red pepper
diet
black water fever
malaria
crunch
in bone
& blood

FOR MY GRANDMOTHER
THINKING OF HER WHILE TEACHING
IN AN ALL BLACK SCHOOL

children at recess
thinking of marcus garvey
in some imperfect song
hold our hands
we are teachers
feeling close to home

in the back rooms
of the school
we say
black is a color
black is me
we love you black people
in africa

when their poems
are birds and spring
my children think
of inchworms
books by langston hughes

PUTTING TIME

putting time
before sixty
into a job

the people
get up
and think
of their children

or dream
of what they
are

before sleep

a woman
sits before
a meal
she did not
have to cook

she is by herself
and does
not miss
the family
she loves

a man
wakes
up   finds
his hands
between
his legs

or goes to sleep
and hears
the darkness
in footsteps
that stop walking

FOR A FRIEND SOMEWHERE

i know when you
fall away
into sleep the countryside
of trees
of empty railway stations
passes beside your face
something tells me
you are moving
through a personal sadness
and reaches over
my eyes
close
like conversation
after too many drinks
how can i tell you
the simple truth
if everything
is an excuse
to avoid
whatever meaning our
words have to say

I SMELL DEATH

i smell death
in a black cat
in a school yard
where children
are too cold
to stand outside
a bored girl
unfolds newspapers
across the sidewalk
and janitors
guard the windows

WHEN YOU LIVE IN THE COUNTRY
YOU STILL HAVE THE FEELING
WE HAVE IN THE CITIES

Cathy ask
    your mother about

      cities
      or small
      open places
      where you can see the snow
      on the mountains
      like
      burlington where

      there are feelings
      that go through
      your skin
      and all the things
      we hide behind
      and under

      being in love
      and poor
      was the way
      i grew
      up in baltimore

      finding the empty
      room
      was only me
      and the books
      i read
      for the words
      that kept
      me

but reading
is only
a dead man
you will get to know

but words
will keep
you through the living
and waiting
you will walk
into

A. PHILIP RANDOLPH

a. philip randolph
six feet
straight

fell like
a board
to the ground

marched for black
people before
i was born

before bigger
thomas
woke up
in the american novel
before
watts
before black men
knew they were
invisible
before cities were places
to leave at evening
before neighborhoods
burned the people
who lived in them
with their own fire
anger
and blackness

FOR PARENTS WHO DO NOT COME TO
PARENTS MEETING AND TEACHERS WHO
TALK ABOUT THE NIGHT

close the door after dark

the shopping centers are hunted
down by young boys
with delicate hands

from house to school
the moonlight makes another
world
of street corner sopranos
cops in sloppy cars
looking for someone to die

WOMEN WALK BECAUSE

women walk because
     airplanes
     drop engines
     into playgrounds
     sea gulls
     fly into air
     conditioners
     meat in cans
     destroys the mind

women walk because men with draft
     cards are tired
     of canada and find
     prison comfortable

women walk because death can
     be a guest at the dinner
     table and clean his plate

women walk because they
     know words are never
     enough when you want to touch

A MINSTREL MAN

a minstrel
man
sings
coon songs
thru
thick (not
his own)
lips
  dies with
        white clothes
on

bert williams
became a clown
got everything
he wanted
bought a glass
of gin fifty
dollars a shot

white gloves
the heart
  of the audience
  on his hands
        in his slow songs

HOW MANY KNEW BESSIE

how many knew bessie bessie before she died
cared enough when she sang
bessie on both sides of the street
singing bessie bringing james baldwin
home bessie bessie smith

WHEN MY GRANDMOTHER DIED

when
my
grandmother
died

a black
bird
was
lost
inside
the
house

FANNIE LOU HAMER

fannie
lou
hamer
never
heard
of
in chicago
was
known for
her
big
black
mouth
in the
south

fannie lou
ate
her greens
watched
her land
and wanted
to
vote

men went
to the bottom
of the river
for wanting less
but fannie
got up
went to the courthouse

big as a fist
black as the ground
underfoot

SCOTT JOPLIN

it is not my music you hear
not the sounds of the streets
returning to us

i have never dressed like louis armstrong
nor heard my music in crowded rooms
i hear the young sing
new songs that can never be music

played loud in cellars
and small apartments
where my people cannot live

MARY'S SCHOOL

we burn logs
use charred splinters
for lead

mash elderberries
for ink

i beg for lamps
and broken
chairs

corn sacks for mattress
spanish moss for mattress hair

black woman
black children live in my heart
africa
is my blood
black children breath
and live

i am my mother's daughter
my life is my people

i have prayed in cotton fields
for a small country school

my life is not africa
my life is my people

africa is a drum
beating in my heart

i am my mother's daughter
writing begging letters

praying in cotton fields
for a small country school

dark as my people
i walk for my children
my school
for i am my mother's daughter
africa is a drum
beating
in my heart

i want the world
for my children

the world i found
when i learned to read

when the scales fell from my eyes
when i learned to read

africa is not my life
my children in cotton fields
dark as the africa
beating in my heart
dark as the skin
of my people

SOME BLACK TEACHERS WHO LOVE
THEIR STUDENTS BEAT THEM TO
DEATH WITH DICTIONARIES

think of the children
they sleep in barber chairs

we are beating them with nouns today
theirs is a language to be forgotten

they need soap and shoes to be quiet at tables
let's give them a proper sound   someday

they will need words to buy bread

WE HAVE NEVER LOVED

we have
never
loved
each other
we
have
only
this house
this street
these neighborhoods
to misunderstand
ourselves
this food
these wages
it is
not love
but
something
deeper
than fear
that makes
you call me
brother
in a strange
city
of white
men

i harriet tubman
black woman
and wife
left my husband
and the south

went north
hidden in manure
or under night
only to find

i left my brothers
my sisters
walking in the fields

filling bags
with cotton
polishing silver

eating beans
and beans
and beans

i went south
again
to find
i was a woman

i went south
and found
i was black

i went south
to be black

HARRIET TUBMAN, HARRIET TUBMAN

harriet tubman
harriet tubman
harriet tubman came down the river in a gunboat
                                    in a gunboat
harriet tubman came down the river

the slaves waited on the shore
the slaves waited on the shore
harriet sing
harriet sing to your people
the captain said harriet sing to your people

there is a home
there is a home
there is a home somewhere
and it ain't over jordan
and it ain't over jordan

harriet sing to your people
there is a home
there is a home somewhere

moses coming
moses coming
harriet tubman the moses of her people

harriet tubman
you are so black
you are so black
harriet tubman you are the moses of your people

IN MAYESVILLE, SOUTH CAROLINA

in mayesville south carolina
i was born last

of seventeen children
in mayesville south carolina

my mother and father africa
their country once slaves now free
of the masters white skin and clothes

had seventeen children
in mayesville south carolina

my mother worked with
my father
picking cotton

washing
ironing

in mayesville south carolina
i was born
my father my father's father
my sisters
africa
our country

MARY MCLEOD BETHUNE

mary mcleod bethune
knows
jane johnson's body knew
and swore
being a woman
is more than
being white
but if you
are black
and a woman
sometimes you have to steal a book
or read in the linen closet
put sand
in your body
when a man looks
at your legs
sometimes you sell
pies to buy
a horse
act dumb
because men forget
they are dealing
with a human being
and put a pistol in your breast

ANN PETRY

a black woman writes of streets

finding a nail in the floor
with her foot

of being alone
in herself
with a family

of the empty heads
of black people in history books

when she fried her hair
and was still black
not wanting to be anything but herself

CAPE COD 2

cape cod
this is something i live with
men asleep on their faces
in the street
the good days of the neighborhood bar
the last fifty cent beer
the comb in the back pockets
of the young
proud of their afros

here my feet on a rail
the free pretzels
and hardboiled eggs
the beer
       is cold
          cold
          cold

and nobody asks
me
about george jackson
or says he is one of the black
students going
to sleep
in the back
of the room

AFRICA CAN NEVER BE AS CLOSE

For Lillian Barbour

africa
can never
be as
close
or remembered
as the
place
my grandmother
died
her body
finished
and pressing
into
the earth

africa
can never
be as
close
as the mother
i cannot
understand
or touch
that loves
me

when i am
alone
and see
no one
africa is not
the dark
i see
but the children
afraid
or angry
waiting
on a corner
that approaches
quickly

I HAVE SEEN MEN

i have seen men
fighting
over paper bags
            their feet
            sheltered against
                        the street
in shoes wrapped
by the new york
            times   cardboard
                        from shirt boxes

i walk over men
who look dead sleeping
            on the buttocks
            of other men
                        for heat for love
                        by touching skin

i see policemen
beating the inner things
            of women
                        in narrow cells

IN BROOKLINE

in brookline
in newton
where the blacks are poor
and the bombs
fall in other countries
it is polite
to hide your mother
when she is old and walking
after midnight
in a thin nightgown

IN A RED DRESS

in a red dress
a woman on her knees
washes a floor
a hundred years ago

she is shaping the life of her children
she thinks as a woman
does of freedom
a dark place in the woods
where the north enters the trees

she wonders if words mean history a woman
losing her children
if reading is a crime

she does not ask for pity
there is a damp rag on the floor

she wipes
in the dress she slept in the dress
she had her children in

she scrubs the floor
does not brush her teeth
she picks them with straws or sticks

she moves on her knees
and watches the ceiling in the water
reflected in the water
everything in her life
is hard like the floor she
touches

the water in her hands
the water is between her legs
her body like a sack of muscle
her hands are dark with water

she wonders about her children
how many children if she could count
pass her fingers
about her body
the words she would find if she could read

she gathers water
like sounds in her head
she kneels
like a slave
in church
like a slave preparing to dance
in front of the pig house
she pretends
to be quiet
her mind is grinding
glass
pissing in the evening meal

ANGELA

angela
should have
been
this woman
with her
books
and pictures
asking
children to write
should
have been
this woman
working
quietly
going
home
after
teaching
me about words
so i would
know
who frederick douglass
is   how to spell
deep river
read a newspaper
about
what city burned
who died
for a case
of pepsi

how many of us live
in one room
can serve
five from a can of campbell's soup
can be as strong
as the words
that are anger
growing
in a boy that is becoming
that is learning
to think
to become a man

JOHN

you return to the light
in dark houses
finding string and sometimes
rocks
only you know about

there are so many houses
where you may live
in silence looking
for other lives

you will drift through classrooms
with pockets of webs and lizards
weak cardboard boxes
with turtles

you will dream through math
of animals
the others ate for lunch
and someone will always
wonder why you feel sad

MARCUS
A STUDENT WHO WRITES BACKWARDS AND SITS
CLOSE TO ME EVEN IF I AM READING DR. SEUSS

he spits
at barber poles
or little girls
on sliding
boards

he keeps
his teachers
in shape
throwing matches
in wastebaskets

when i open
a book
pointing
to a picture
of a barn
or street corner

he sits beside me
and tries
to talk

his eyes are still
and he seems to say
how do people live like this

FANNY KEMBLE

up and down
the river
listening

the banjo
black
men singing
rowing

up and down
the river

fanny kemble
heard the blues

MIDWEST 71

in the bar
men roll
cigarettes

watch out
for women

who might
disturb

a game
of pool

the land is clear
enough to see

howard johnsons
five miles away

a woman planting
greens can look
and see the sky

before she sees
a man entering a kitchen

MISSISSIPPI JOHN HURT

mississippi john hurt
a little man
rings around his eyes
big hat
that he took off
to say hello

mississippi john
plays
wearing a vest
a round black hat
a little man
mr hurt
rings under his eyes

sings
a man behind a mule
sings as he works
a little man
works as he sings
mississippi john
big eyed
mississippi john

WE HAVE NEVER BEEN KIND TO WOMEN

we have never
been kind
to women

have left
our cereal bowls
and shirts

walked out
of the house
and mornings

leaving only
what we cared
to give

quickly at night

we have never
been men
for women   have been men
for each other

words about sports
or mountains to climb
even claimed beer
for
us   for our sons

GENERAL

general
the bodies
of the dead
lie
side
by side
colored
dead
seven dollars
a month
regardless
of rank
lie side
by side
with
the union dead

BLACK REGIMENT

col shaw
threw his cigar
away
died at the head
of his troop
or in the ditch
said
with his niggers

not for freedom
but just to live
black soldiers
in the war
unpaid
underpaid
the south saw
them slaves
the north
saw them
three dollars
less than
white

frederick douglass
said
take the war
to africa
but lincoln
worried about runaways
& rebellions

THE ARMY

the army
makes men

of slaves
my grandfather

wore

a uniform
to tuskegee

years after
the war

I GIVE WHAT THERE IS TO GIVE

i give what there is to give

living through winters
tired of my own body

how do we enter such dark lives

wake up in our own

FREDERICK DOUGLASS 2

frederick douglass did you see your mother
did you know the woman in the dark
who said she was your mother
who said she was your mother
is this the woman you remember
the woman you saw only twice
the woman who walked all night
            who walked all night
to see her son   the mother
      walked all night
frederick douglass did you see your mother
did you know the woman
who said she was your mother

how did she know you
how did she know you
did she know you in the dark
did she know the touch of your face
did she know the dark of your face
did she say to herself
this is my son
this is my son
                  frederick
                  frederick douglass did you see
your mother

would you know your mother
would you know your mother
now that you are old
now that you are old
would know the woman who said
     i am your mother
the woman who walked all night
         who walked all night
frederick douglass did you see your mother
did you know the woman in the dark

SOJOURNER TRUTH

sojourner truth
knew the bible that others read

sojourner truth
was a woman having children

sojourner lived
the life of a slave

sojourner truth
met mr lincoln
never knew what he said

sojourner truth was a black woman
lived the life of a slave
who knew the truth as a slave
     knew the bible that others read

when she gave lincoln her photograph
when she gave lincoln her photograph

when he asked her to sign
when he asked her sign   she said i can't
                         i can't

sojourner truth lived the life of a slave
she knew a few words and could not read

mr lincoln
mr lincoln don't you know a slave can't read
mr lincoln don't you know a slave can't read

GEORGE JACKSON

george jackson

we are reading your letters
in class today

the young black children
are talking
while the teacher turns the page

she speaks of guns
there is silence
in the room

i tell them about your mother
and there
is love
& understanding in a schoolroom

Designed by Frank R. DiFederico.
Typeset by Eileen Peterson.
Printed by Universal Lithographers, Inc.